Oleeya,

With all my love

Evelyn Whitebear

1/14

Dancing Between Shadows

Poetry Reflections

---

by Evelyn White-Bey

Produced by:

FriesenPress

Suite 300 – 852 Fort Street
Victoria, BC, Canada V8W 1H8

www.friesenpress.com

Distributed to the trade by The Ingram Book Company

To Mom, with all my love.

Table of Contents

Foreword

When Evelyn asked if I would write some comments for her book of poetry I was reticent. Poetry is a gift absent from my storehouse; prose is much more my comfort-zone. However, because I admire Evelyn so much, with a tinge of reluctance, I agreed to at least consider it. Thus, I suggested she send me the manuscript, so I could see what transpired. Within moments, an interesting juxtaposition of our normal perspective of linear time occurred. Inspiration began to flow straight away as to what I should write. This, the day before her text arrived!

How could this be happening? How could I write any authentic, from-the-heart comments on something I had not even seen? But I have learnt over the years not to ignore inspiration when it starts to flow. If we ignore it, it dries up; if we acknowledge it, it flows sweetly, with often delightfully astonishing results. So, stifling my feelings of hypocrisy I started typing what was flowing into my mind, knowing of a certainty that this was from a place somewhere well beyond my conscious mind.

The next day I read what Evelyn had sent me, and realized every word I had written the previous day accurately reflected my response to what she had sent me. I was very pleased, gratified; I knew from long experience that when inspiration comes in so promptly, so clearly, so unequivocally, it has always proved to be

right – perfect for the situation. This was the first time it had *preceded* the unfold-
ing events like this. But eternity – the source of inspiration – is not limited by the
restrictions we place upon ourselves by the belief in linear time. In eternity there
is only *Now*.

Here is what I wrote:

Poetry is the soul, expressing itself. Some of us can express ourselves best by
actions, some with pictures, some by the spoken word, others by the written
word in prose form and yet others through poetry. In many ways poetry can be
the *most* expressive because it can be at multiple levels at once; some literal, some
allegorical, some mystical or esoteric.

So often, poetry can be involuntarily thought-provoking. Poetry is best, most
expressive when it is written under inspiration. Inspiration means 'in the spirit'.
In this state the soul of the poet is able to bring through depths and heights and
breadths of meanings from the most profound and sublime to the mundane. It
can even incongruously, yet somehow meaningfully, intermingle all these quali-
ties at once, bringing new understanding to ideas that the reader may previously
have not discerned. Is this not a gift, a prompting from the Divine Spirit that
lives within the innermost part of us all?

One can read prose without making a connection with its source, but to appreci-
ate poetry a resonance must become established with the mind, the soul of its
author. Evelyn's poetry did this to me without me being aware it was happening.
It shows a rarely expressed insightfulness of the 'little things' that, woven together,
form a tapestry of conjoined fragments that make up our life's experiences and
help the more reflective amongst us grow spiritually.

Deeply poignant, penetrating, enthralling, this labor of love just gets better and
better as we progress through it. I could tell – and you will, too – that Evelyn
simply *had* to write this. There is a message – at *least* one! – for us all within these
pages. When I finished reading Evelyn's amazing, picture-evoking words, I was
glad I had read it; not missed it. And I rejoiced. I believe you will, too.

Brian Longhurst

Author, "Seek ye First the Kingdom…" One man's journey with the living Jesus.

Evelyn White-Bey

Introduction

Dancing Between Shadows: Poetry Reflections is a collection of poems written over several years. The poems reflect memories ranging through domestic violence, childhood challenges, love, pain, romance, nature, death and spirituality. These experiences have been my best teachers and they are the ingredients that make up these poems. During my periods of writing, there were outbursts of illumined inspiration and, at other times, dark nothings. These poems could be short stories condensed into poetry form.

My mother will always be the strongest woman I know. She struggled through hardship and challenges most of her life, yet never gave up. This book is dedicated to her. She played the hand the Universe dealt her.

Her love silent, yet
arms so strong and wide
to encircle nine children
leaving out none.
Her discontent
shielded from her young,
who were always scrambling
for a mother's affection.

I pray that I gain an ounce of my mother's strength to pass down to my children and grandchildren and their children. She has a precious, rare quality; not everyone possesses that ability.

Poetry has been my hushed lover since I was a little girl. For me, poetry provided a route of escapism; it disconnected me from reality, dropping me into a make-believe space where I could do anything or be anybody. Writing poetry is how I endured the difficult times.

I grew up in rural North Carolina with eight siblings. My father was a sharecropper and the breadwinner of the family. We lived on various farms owned by the "bossman." Since the houses we lived in were owned by the "bossman," it was required that families work on the farm. There were no written contracts; there were no options. If you refused to work on the farm, you had better start looking for another home. That is how it was.

My father worked hard to provide for a large family. There was always the possibility of not having enough to eat and often that was the case. Other times, my father could not pay the monthly rent and subsequently forced to move. Like nomads, we moved around a lot. We were regularly changing schools, sometimes two or three times in a single semester. We met other classmates in schools but rarely did we remain long enough to make friends.

Many of the poems written during school are long gone. My high-school English teacher asked me what I wished to be when I grew up and I excitedly told her that I would be a poet. She sneered and stated, "You can't make money being a poet." That was a crushing blow and for many years, I stopped writing. Little did the teacher know that money was not as important as enjoying something that generated joy. Anyway, I threw out my poems, which was a mistake because I felt they would be no use to me later in life. My one regret: I allowed this teacher to wound me, but at least she did not kill my dream.

I loved reading works of poets such as Emily Dickinson, Elizabeth Barrett Browning, Robert Frost, and Langston Hughes. I must admit though that during my young years, I did not quite grasp the larger concepts behind

Evelyn White-Bey

their writing. The understanding would come later when my attitude and writing took on a serious tone. For obvious reasons, I gravitate towards writers with similar experiences: hardships, difficulties, emotional upheavals, and disappointments.

I enjoy reading poetry by Gwendolyn Brooks. Brooks, who grew from humble beginnings, wrote such blessed poetry, such as, "Speech to the Young: Speech to the Progress-Toward", "Kitchenette Building", and "The Bean Eaters."

David Whyte is another poet whom I admire. His style of writing resonates with me. I often reflect upon his words, "The discipline of poetry is in over-hearing yourself say difficult truths from which it is impossible to retreat. Poetry is a break for freedom." Some of my favorites are, "The Opening of the Eye", "Faith", "The Lightest Touch", and "Everything Is Waiting for You."

I am thankful for the hard lessons; they have humbled me. I am thankful for God's mercy to be here to share my poetry with you. My sincere gratitude to you, who provided support, read my poems, listened, wrote comments, offered criticisms, and performed editorial remarks. Today, poetry continues to serve as a refuge when I desire to withdraw from the noisy hustle and bustle.

I would say to anyone who has uncovered their passions to follow them wherever they lead. Many may not like what you do, but never allow that to hinder you from pursuing your dreams.

Acknowledgements

This book is dedicated to my mother and late father, who presented me with the experiences to write my story. Without you, this book could not have been written. To my husband, Jan, and sons, Adrian and Hammed—you provided love, reassurance, constructive criticisms, and always believed in me. To Sharon Alexander—you are my spiritual sister and the incredible artist who designed my book cover. To Ilich A. Briones—you became my sounding board, confidant and offered insight and consolation whenever I became stuck or frustrated. To Ann Knight-Davis, Lynn Dean, Jennifer Pew, Sandy Hall, and Suzanne Hudgens—you looked beyond the flaws and saw only beauty in the work I was endeavoring to breathe into existence. To Philip Hubbard, a fellow poet (who recently transitioned)—his appreciation of my work will always inspire me. I thank Carol Romano and Darlene Dumpit--you both contributed immensely to the book with your editing expertise. To my siblings and their families—you have become my loudest and proudest cheerleaders. Close friends (too numerous to mention) have and continue to keep me centered and grounded. You all have my unconditional love.

Dancing Between Shadows

Like a heavy overcoat,
my countenance emptied of light,
sinking in mire of unworthiness.
Memories stalking, dragging me
to familiar dwellings of discontent,
where childhood pleasures robbed.
Scars of fear and shame
but,
the rhapsody of music
pulsates in my head.
Slowly I begin to sway.
I dance … my pain abates
… breathing returns
… dreams within reach.

I dance
when slumbering souls rest.
In deep-rooted darkness
I dance under twilight,
escaping haunting shadows.
So, reaching up,
grasping the moon's etheric fingers,
I dance to healing arias of Saturn
… to descants of Heaven
… to flutists of the Navajo.

I dance,
in refuge of swirling movement,

Evelyn White-Bey

inhaling incenses of jasmine.
Briefly, I dared to smile.
I dance, my heart thumps to the rhythm of drums.
I dance in the saddle of winter's wind.
I dance in the shadows of bygone diaries.

My mind elopes to Eden,
where none can enter.
An angel's wings enfold me and
I dance
to stringed instruments by waiting sages,
whose gleeful air
makes me swoon.
I dance beneath clouds of starry galaxies,
piercing shadows.
I dance in soulful harmony.
I dance in the shadow of grace.

I dance on winged musical chords,
shirking a branded past,
momentarily.
I dance, I am dancing
between shadows.

Relations

Genealogy

Vibrant swatches of mismatched fabrics,
cut from children's
worn out checkered-board,
flannel pajamas.
Burlap dresses
that itched and pinched.
Dated, faded cotton plaid shirts,
polyester knits,
frayed, over-washed blue jeans,
Jimmy's textile tossed surplus scraps,
checkered boxer underwear,
ripped ruffle petticoats,
vintage European linen tablecloths,
hand-me-down draperies,
embroidered handkerchiefs,
a salvaged azure polka-dotted dress.
Whimsical patterns of country farmhouses,
red chanticleers,
purple elephants,
evergreens,
seen-better-days lighthouses,
scarlet roses,
rustic teakettles,
fused patterns fraught,
stitched together with
assorted threads,

Evelyn White-Bey

weaving in and
through,
becoming elaborately woven
one-of-a-kind tapestries,
ancestral hand-made keepsakes.

Mattie

People praised Mattie for being strong.
Jimmy, her husband, my uncle,
after forty years of marriage,
suffered a fatal heart attack.
No one saw a tear
fall from Mattie's hazel eyes.
People said Mattie
was resilient.
Through the service,
burial,
even the repast with its huge gathering
of family, friends, and strangers,
Aunt Mattie smiled, greeted, hugged and
kissed everyone.
She consoled, served and
laughed out loud.
A gracious host was she.
Still people cried,
not Mattie.
Not a tear did people see her shed.
All believed she was tough;
a courageous woman.
When all traces of family,
friends and strangers had departed,
what they didn't see was
Aunt Mattie
alone,
crying in the dark.

Evelyn White-Bey

Yesterday

Mother,
pregnant again.
A farmer father worked
for miniscule pay,
trespassing at night,
stealing food under
mantle of blackness.
Days, sometimes,
nine siblings,
empty stomachs,
not enough to eat.
Growling, gnawing aches.
So many mouths to feed.
Jammed into a four-room house--
a shotgun house, folks called it.
Tiny bodies pressed together in three beds.
No running water, no inside toilet,
no furnace.
Winters were brutal,
summers worse.
The constant battle swatting flies,
damn them flies.
Gnats, mosquitoes, and
bed bugs
that crawled inside wood walls,
onto burlap sheets,
pillows,
sucking blood

from puny flesh,
scampering at daybreak.
Homes full of cracks and holes,
frigid wind found its way
into our scrawny bodies,
into our bones.
An indelible past
that won't die.

Evelyn White-Bey

Memories

We lived in shoddy houses.
The family moved a lot,
two or three times a year.
After thirty years
we travelled back,
revisiting some of them.
Most were torn down, burned,
some collapsed, few remained.
One in particular stood out,
beckoning me.
What seemed a castle
was no more than a four-room house,
too small for our expanding family.
Windows replaced
by weather-aged plywood,
rotting columns,
sagging beneath a tin roof.
Rickety porch, missing boards,
screen door swinging
back and forth on rusted hinges.
Inside, mildewy dankness,
linoleum tile worn bare
exposing course splintered wood.
Light fixtures bare,
colored wires dangling
like skinny limbs.
Surrounded by clumps of dirt fields
where green crops used to be.

Red barn and silo lay in rubble.
Now,
Sparrows, crows and seagulls parade.
Remembering
the timid and shy little girl
who played hide and seek
with shadows and fleeting dreams.
Fragmented joys,
muffled secrets.

Evelyn White-Bey

Awareness

Living under weight of domestic violence
it was difficult to understand how
one person who professed to love
could also hurt. Alcohol and other
addictions hurt loved ones
on many levels,
leaving ineffaceable scars that never
fade or heal. I know, I carry them
every day. Scars become
incessant reminders of a traumatic and
darkened past. Wounded,
I carry the pain of past injuries.
Although at times, I succeed in
shoving them back to the dark
crannies of my mind, but like a
boomerang, always
finding their way back—teasing,
tempting me to again experience
the fear. Thoughts hover
at the rim of my consciousness.
When I shine light, confronting them,
they scurry like moths at dawn
taunting and teasing,
never gone; simply masked.

Instability

My youngest son,
always tripping,
falling over his tiny,
awkward feet.
Surprised, entangled,
he'd stare up at me
from the ground and
wonder what happened.
I'd take his hand, help him up.
Several steps later
it happens again.
His feet become twisted and
down he'd go,
like plump rocks in water.
I'd catch him sometimes,
just before he'd fall.
I'd see the jiggle,
teeter–totter,
as he'd start to lean.
Other times he just flopped,
rolled, or tumbled.
Completely perplexed
he'd gaze at his lil bitty feet
as if something was amiss.
He'd point to his feet,
scolding,
reprimanding,
"You behave!"

Evelyn White–Bey

They didn't, so
he kept falling.
He'd look up at me
knowing I would
pick him up.
I always did.

Relations

Ann and I
treasure simple things.
We can laugh
at the drop of a dime.
We observe something and,
without saying a word,
burst into howls of laughter.
We laugh so hard
tears spill down our cheeks,
our sides ache.
At times, we can't catch our breath.
Ann will call to say, "Ok, I need to laugh."
Quickly, searching my mind,
I snatch a funny memory and,
just like that,
it starts.
We don't talk much, we just laugh
about things that transpired
years ago,
like the man in a talent show,
who thought he was a famous singer
with too many facial contortions and
bulging, blaring eyes.
Or the man asleep on the bus,
whose head was jerking up and down
as if bobbing for apples.
Or my grandmother, whose
vocabulary consisted of non-existent words--

Evelyn White-Bey

we laughed behind her back.
Or the silly things we did,
reliving the traumatic and
comedic events of our lives.
Laughter,
a soothing embrace.

Secrets

Her entire life,
like a sponge
absorbing and taking on
others woes, sorrows, but
ever smiling, forgiving
unnecessarily.
She became clever at
hiding emotions,
stuffing them in Grandma's
canning jars
filled with sweet
fruit preserves.

Evelyn White-Bey

Strength

(by my siblings)
My mother, now
like a tree, towering,
statuesque,
flexible,
resilient,
alive.
Years ago, she was frail,
troubled,
vulnerable,
scared.
Mother endured
unimaginable pain,
suffering, abuse.
not by hands of strangers,
but by hands of a
man she trusted.
If only she could have seen
what lay ahead.
An ill-fated future racing head-on.
But, at nineteen,
how could she have known?
A dream clearly within sight
would rudely end.
Then we began to
Inhale,
exhale.
We breathed life into our

mother's body
when she contemplated giving up.
We gave her reasons to live;
death would not rob her.
For our every two heartbeats,
one beat for her.
Every cut, bruise,
we washed, cleansed, healed
her darkened wounds.
For every goal she failed to achieve
we created windows of opportunity.
We breathed for our mother
when she wanted to quit
breathing.
For every tear shed
we tenderly wiped away.
During deep depression,
we raised her up
from a grave of hopelessness.
For every strike upon her body,
unselfishly we absorbed her pain,
lessening the impact.
Mother, humbled by her experiences,
never cursed the darkness
nor lost her infectious smile.
Our mother has recovered and
rediscovered her will to live.

Evelyn White-Bey

Oppression

No puddle,
stream,
lake,
river,
sea, or
ocean,
could ever hold
the amount of tears my mother shed
through years
of violence, humiliation,
abuse
from a man who
everyday said,
"I love you."

Remorse

So clearly I remember
the baritone voice of my father
barking orders. We'd scatter,
racing to get it done,
not wanting to ignite his anger.
For many years we lived with that voice,
the voice of my father.
I saw only the bad,
the authoritative, dictatorial side.
A gentle side surfaced at times.
Underneath his solid armor of flesh and bones
there was a caring man.
Rarely did I acknowledge the good,
like the beautiful vegetable gardens
he grew year after year that sustained us
or the way he stuck out his chest
when he spoke proudly of his children,
or how he always found shelter
for a growing family,
or his courage portrayed in
challenging situations.
He was fearless,
but I didn't mention them,
not until he died unexpectedly.
No time to say all those things

Evelyn White-Bey

I should have spoken.
He gave all he had,
that was what he knew.
It was enough!

Detachment

For years,
I held them.
I hugged and loved them,
each their own personality.
Many days of play, pranks,
young innocence.
I protected them from
distractions
that loitered around dark corners,
awaited them on the streets.
Time sped up, caught me unawares,
and one by one they left.
I remember the ache,
heavy upon my breast,
at losing my precious ones
to life.
I cried for that which
I could never keep,
but will always hold.

Evelyn White-Bey

Worthy

I am a child of God, so you will not:

lie to me,
swear at me,
control my life,
accuse me falsely,
take me for granted,
use me as a punching bag,
stab me with a steak knife,
steal my crumbs of solace,
sever my dreams, aspirations,
touch me without permission,
destroy my personal belongings,
take your frustrations out on me,
disrespect me publicly or privately,
shoot at me while fleeing from you,
use alcohol as an excuse to abuse me,
call me anything other than my name,
order me around as if I am your child,
buy alcohol before feeding your family,
place the sole of your shoe on my backside,
slap me with your exposed palm or knotted fist,
blacken my eyes to keep me locked in the shadows,
kick me out of my home in winter with children in tow.
No, you will treat me as the amazing human being that I AM.
I deserve nothing less.

Abyss

Aesthetically cleaned, whiffs of Lysol,
colorless walls, blotchy white tiles.
In a corner Grandmother sits,
eyes fixed on a multicolored quilt,
familiarity teasing, dancing along the hems
of her grayish wrinkled brain and purplish veins,
phasing out of focus and in.
A skeletal frame veiled in teal medical garments,
shrinking in an oversized faux leather chair.
A wisp of silvery hair escapes her bun, unnoticed.
Head tilted, listening to nameless voices.
She breathes between the spaces, pauses
of consciousness and oblivion,
perplexity and isolation.
Scrawny fingers claw air of invisible phantoms,
struggling to retain glimpses of identity.
Her mind dims like dreams that
dissipate upon wakening.
Chatoyant amber eyes, misty, glossless.
Forgetfulness, like a shroud,
swathes her countenance.
Aged cocoa leathery skin,
baked by summer's oven.
Hollow cheeks, deep crevices and crinkles,
where memories hide, inaccessible.

Evelyn White-Bey

A weak, feeble body, but
sturdy hands clutch mine,
pleading for tiny jewels of remembrance.
Darkness shadows recollections.
Where memories blazed,
only smoldering embers remain.

Bittersweet

Poorly knitted,
hand-me-down ecru cardigan,
hung loosely on his
gangly frame.
His eyes shielded.
Sighing,
he heaved a soiled pillowcase
over his scrawny shoulder
filled with measly belongings.
Worn Brogan shoes
shuffled across the
depressed green
vinyl kitchen tile to the open door.
Thinking he'd change his mind
he stood several seconds,
his back towards me,
head slouched.
His pride too great to include me;
shame too strong to face me,
he'd rather die than fail.
My lover departed.
He shoved open the
tattered screen door,
stepping into a,
moonless-lit sky.

Evelyn White-Bey

Darkness swallowed him.
Faintly,
I caught the sound of his shoes
scraping across stone and sand.

Masked

Who will I be
today?
Tomorrow?
Anybody.
Everybody.
Like you,
I wear masks,
hiding the real me.
Not one sees me as I am,
only what I allow them to see.
And, it is a lie.
It is not me!

Concealed behind fabricated smiles
sympathetic rhetoric, I am
perpetrating a fraud.
Like a chameleon
I alter, camouflage, color
myself to fool you.
I imitate you.
I am master of creative disguises.
I am you, and you me.
Think you know who I am?
You can't ever know me.
I don't know me.
What am I? Who am I?
An imposter!

Evelyn White-Bey

Counterfeit,
a smokescreen of deception
is all that I display.
People say they love me,
but, who is "me" they love?
Don't be deceived.
What you see is an act,
a charade.
I am somewhere
concealed beneath layers
of hardened veneer.
Smothered.
Asphyxiated.
I am a sham
playing a role
that is not mine.

Pretentious I can be.
stringing imaginary airs
I masquerade about
flaunting a fake.
I am not real.
Me! Me!
Where am I?
Buried deep in creases,
between layers of
ancient skin
and time.

Who am I?

I hide myself well
I can be anybody,
except me.
You and me wear disguises,
we fear authenticity.
So, we live in a world filled
with pretenders, impersonators,
and I
fit right in.
Shielded by our masks,
we are all imposters!

Evelyn White-Bey

Liberated

She is free.
A tumultuous journey
no more.
Like an unopened rose
confined in
its bud,
imprisoned
inside a crypt of
unspeakable
grief.
Then,
waltzes in freedom
waving her
triumphant
banner.
Now,
a delicate rose
materializes,
petals unfolding,
limbs stretching
upwards
towards the
infinite face
of God.

Trials

Friday night.
Gusty winds
rattle windows,
tremble our skinny bodies.
His voice thunderous
angry, threatening.
Hers, pleading, softer.
We lie awake fully clothed
beneath hand-made quilts.
Drafty rooms sucking out heat
Shoes line up at side of bed
knowing any moment
we have to jump into them.
We lie awake
Listening for the moment
when we must run.
I hold my sisters hand
beneath the heavy covers
comforting them.
My older brother whispers,
"Get ready."
A mastered routine;
we know what he means.
Be quick or get caught.
Hearing the first strike
we spring up,
jump in shoes.
Eyes wide, darting wildly

Evelyn White-Bey

in the semi-darkness.
A door bangs.
That's our cue.
We sprint out the side door
leaping over concrete steps,
hitting the ground like gazelles
seeking shelter temporarily
in the waiting forest,
praying that morning
breathes a sober
soul.

Evelyn White-Bey

Life

Ambiguity

Uncertainty hangs
like an ominous cloud,
mirroring our every thought
as we sluggishly grind
towards an uncertain future.
Ensnared in vise of
corruptibility,
its grasp constricting,
choking reality,
as we live under
shrouds of deceit,
inundated with the task
of disentangling truth
from falsehood.
The once
gaudy voices of right,
silenced by legislative
commandments.
So we endure
forfeiture of control,
stifle-ness,
weak-kneed
mindless
nobodies,
moseying through life
like blind sheep
herded into slaughter.

Evelyn White-Bey

Pity

Poor
penniless
peddlers
paddle through
privileged rubbles
for pieces of worthy
pickings,
sifting through
putrid debris
of day-old purging
while the pious and
pretentious prattle
from their pristine
parlors, pointing at
prudishness of
the poor.
Pity them,
the pathetic,
passionless people.

Mindfulness

Mind your business,
people on my street,
don't speak.
They keep to themselves.
Coming from where I'm from,
our business was everybody's.
But the people on my street
fade into shadows, retreating.
People on my street
blind, legally blind
to sunlit crimes.
How can I ask for help
when they have no eyes to see
what's happening on their street
or see even me?
People on my street
have lost the courage to speak.
Their tongues unmoving,
lips sealed,
while laws are created and passed.
People on my street have
lost their voices of reason.
People on my street don't hear
beautiful sounds of nature.
Beauty of a child's laughter--quiet.
Songs of a lark—hushed.

Evelyn White-Bey

People on my street
shut out the melodies of Earth.
People on my street are dead.
I moved.

Gratitude

Upon awakening today
I said, "thank you."
Some didn't rise.
On my travels to work
I said, "thank you."
Some didn't make it.
For my meals
I whispered, "thank you."
Many are hungry.
For my health, my body,
so grateful I am, "thank you."
Some are ill.
For my breath, my lungs,
I shouted, "thank you!"
Some breathe with respirators.
For my eyes, my sight,
I chanted, "thank you."
Some are blind.
For peace of mind,
"thank you."
Many are restless.
For good friends,
"thank you."
Many are alone.
For my children, my family,
"thank you."
Some are grieving a loss.

Evelyn White-Bey

Prophets

When I think about good in this world,
you come to mind.
When I think about perseverance and tolerance,
I think of you because you are
one of the most tolerant people I know.
You have been, and still are, tried and tested
by those who think they are different and better.
When I think of fearlessness and courage,
I think of you, as your journey is a lonely one.
Under the cloak of darkness, many nights
you shed tears, pray, ask why.
I say, hold on.
When I think of an indomitable will,
I think of you.
The pressure is at times disheartening.
When I think of strength,
I think of you with many formidable tasks
that lay upon you and before you.
When I think about challenges and oppositions,
I think about you.
You are relentlessly and shamelessly
confronted in a difficult arena.
When I think of kindness and compassion,
I think of you.
The debates at times are unpleasant, disrespectful.
When I think about resolution,
I think of you, your undaunted faith.
I say, hold on.

When I think about courage,
I think of you.
Even while others vilify you,
you find the spirit to smile.
When I think of integrity,
I think of you, as you refuse to be persuaded,
your principles intact.
When I think about heroes and role models,
I think of you.
Many look up to you.
When I think of hope
HOPE
I think of you, as you give our young inspiration,
encouragement, reasons to honor goals.
When I think about devotion and commitment,
I think of you because of your duty to God, not man.
I think of you because you
were destined before birth to take a leading role
to create unity among all people,
birth light where there is none,
open closed hearts,
sprinkle joy on Earth,
hammer peace into souls of humanity.
Thank God for anointing you.
Thank God for your existence.
You are a star that shines,
giving all permission to do the same.
I say shine, shine, shine.

Evelyn White-Bey

There are others who refuse to praise, only criticize,
show not gratitude, but arrogance,
give not respect, but malice,
convey not kindness, but condemnation.
I say, hold on.
Thank you for preserving your integrity.
Thank you for not making quitting an option.
Thank you for being a gladiator.
Thank you for living your truth,
knowing your truth is our truth.
Thank you for acknowledging the ancestors,
who blazed trails before us;
we all are pieces cut from the same tapestry.
You are the epitome of love;
others talk it, you walk it.
Some preach it, you live it.
Finally,
I say hold on,
HOLD on.

Equality

To those who erect our prestigious
colleges and universities of higher learning,
who will never step foot in one.
No money for tuition.
To those who sew designer clothing, footwear,
who will not be able to buy them,
 unable to wear what they make.
To those who build mansions,
mortar by mortar, brick by brick,
who will never live in the
 homes they construct.
Minimum wage.
To those who tirelessly work
long hours to make luxury autos,
who will never own them
unable to drive the finished product.
To those who helped build this land,
through sweat and struggle,
who have no voice;
their stories omitted from history.

Evelyn White-Bey

Insanity

Today

>I read to a blind woman,
>I emptied my neighbor's trash,
>I helped my son with his math,
>I called a friend who recently had surgery,
>but I didn't make the early news.
>No front page headlines;
>that's reserved for criminals.

Yesterday

>I held a door for an elderly man,
>I helped a child onto a bus,
>I helped a motorist with a flat tire,
>I listened to someone's grieving story,
>but I didn't make the evening news.
>No award of honor,
>that's reserved for entertainers.

Tomorrow

>I will gladly give someone my seat,
>I will give smiles to strangers,
>I will pray for the mother,
>who lost a child,
>I will feed the hungry,
>clothe the homeless,
>but I will not make the late news,
>no special ceremony.
>That's reserved for politicians.

Superstition

A letter rests
upon my mantle,
sealed tightly,
unopened.
A scarlet envelope,
with familiar handwriting
scrawled in indigo ink.
Longing to open,
it rests between my fingers.
Caressing, stroking,
imagining the touch
of one who sent it.
Mingled with regret and nostalgia,
when old thoughts come
rushing back,
the past catching up with me,
back onto the mantle it went.
Without warning,
a breeze
wafts through
an open door,
tossing my scarlet letter
from its resting place,
falling, drifting pass my outstretched hands
into the flaming pit below.
Burning, charring,
It's secret sealed inside sealed
unopened.

Evelyn White-Bey

Mississippi

With some effort,
I pushed truth of past
out of my mind.
It hurts too much to revisit,
but truth kept returning
again to the south--
Mississippi.
A few years ago I traveled there.
The energy of the place touched me
before the wheels of the plane skidded on the runway.
Shadowy souls of the past rose up to greet me.
I traveled through towns of Mississippi,
staring at strong, tall maple and oak trees that
reminded me of muscular, sturdy Africans.
I wondered which slaves had been hung
from hundreds of aged trees
after being beaten with whips and chains.
I saw their bodies,
glistened and bloodied in the noonday summer sun.
I saw trees with its lower branches missing and
I thought about branches
breaking from dead weight
or, perhaps Mississippi had sawed off
limbs to remove traces
of her past travesty and shame.
There, accusers stood with their children,
laughing brazenly as human beings died
from strangulation, suffocation.

I turned away,
saddened by visions of broken necks,
disfigured and mutilated bodies.
I saw men, women, and children
walking along the shoulder of a highway.
A few years ago,
many were shot for sport,
slogging their weary bodies home after
cleaning houses,
laboring in fields till dark.
Nursing babies,
babies not from their wombs,
preparing hot meals not for their tables,
fighting the growing itch to rebel.
I traveled past a town square
that still displayed an auction block
where they sold human beings
for little money to the highest bidder
or traded for livestock or food.
I imagine their flesh groped, fondled,
squeezed, pinched,
as if pieces of fruit.
Humiliation and shame visible on their faces,
pain reflected in their frozen tears.
I saw a minister on a church stoop,
speaking to a small congregation.
Not long ago his tongue would have been ripped out
or whipped until bloodied flesh

Evelyn White-Bey

looked like shredded ribbons
for merely preaching the Gospel.
Reading was a luxury
reserved not for them.
I saw families walking together.
They would have been
separated and sold like cattle
to different owners
across the country.
I thought about the women
who gave birth to children,
only to have them sold and
never to be seen again.
My heart ached.
Gritting my teeth, I fought urge to vomit
and spit upon the soil of the south.
I remembered my ancestors,
I saw their backs, bent and broken
from lengthy days and nights of toil.
I heard their cries for justice, liberty, freedom,
and rest . . . sweet, sweet rest.
Lips mumbling in silent prayer
for better tomorrows
intended for their children and
their children's children, so
the ancestors endured.
Mississippi was unkind to its tenants.
Atrocities of its past haunt the town,

scrambling to keep truth hidden.
No warmth greeted me as I traveled its ghostly streets.
The chilly breaths of past inhabitants breathed upon my neck,
beseeching me to avenge their suffering.
Mississippi carries their souls,
ghost-bound to land,
unable to free themselves and
escape miseries of yesterday.
The injustices tattooed upon Mississippi's face,
seared into its bones.
Restless souls moving through streets,
houses, fields, trees,
seeking redemption, peace.
I tried to avert my eyes
but their pain was in me,
in my body, my soul, my bones.
I left Mississippi, shortening my stay,
cries of slaves' deafening
pain mingling with my own,
pressure of the past, too strong to ignore.
The stench of burning flesh seared my nostrils,
making my eyes hemorrhage,
waking my senses to a history never told,
will never be told.
Nooses clutching broken necks,
barefoot, uneducated children who
haven't known a world beyond captivity.

Evelyn White-Bey

My ancestors,
deprived of justice, hope, and opportunity.
People without a prayer.
Mississippi should be on its knees.

Tomorrow

Winds blow,
taking with it
yesterday,
leaving
vague
memories
of a past.
Still
winds blow,
pushing me
with it
into tomorrow,
leaving
little time to
remember
today.

Evelyn White-Bey

Desire

Duality

Onions make me cry,
       but not tomatoes.
Pepper makes me sneeze,
       but not salt.
Rum makes me drunk,
       but not lemonade.
Poison ivy makes me itch,
       but not wild honeysuckle.
Old romantic movies make me blue,
       but not you.
Never you.

Evelyn White-Bey

Retrospect

Looking back,
he wished he'd been smarter and
not given in to temptation.
He wished he had simply let her go
to seek future endeavors,
but shared a secret,
should have kept silent.
Opening Pandora's ebony box,
he wished he could change,
take it all back,
left things the way they were.
He shouldn't have met her
one warm afternoon
for a brief city adventure.
He wished he could have been stronger and
taken her hand away when
she gently held his.
He wished he'd said no when she asked for a kiss
but he yielded and shuddered.
He should have walked away, not looked back.
He was weak, too weak to leave.
Passion burned a hole in his soul,
relentless, she was
breaking him down
down.
He wished he had pushed her hands away
when she caressed his face.
He wished she had not touched

the sensuous nape of his neck
that caused his senses to amplify.
He wished he had fought her off,
shoved her away.
He wished things could go back
to the way they used to be.
He wished he hated her warm embraces
wrapped tightly around him
that took his breath away,
igniting flames he thought had died.
He wished he'd been stronger and
walked away,
instead he anxiously awaited
another touch,
another kiss of sin.

Passion

Handsome man,
dance with me quickly,
before the song ends.
Let your guard down,
dapper man,
let it drop
like old yesterdays.
Take my hand,
while we dance.
Hold me closer,
beautiful man, closer.
Let me feel your breath
upon my scented cheek
as I inhale your masculinity.
Fine, fine man,
let me touch your face,
kiss your sensual mouth,
before your woman
comes looking.

Fire

His eyes
dazzled like
meticulously
polished diamonds,
mirroring
noonday sun,
glittering,
sparkling.
Yearning
did I desire to
pluck them out
and plant
them in
fertile soil to sprout
replicas,
shed light
in dark crevices
of my tormented mind.

Evelyn White-Bey

Reminiscence

Seedy neighborhood,
a dank jazzy soul joint where
crooning down-home locals mingle.
Jazz musicians congregate
under a canopy of blackness.
Jukebox rhythms,
fingers snapping,
feet tapping,
bodies swishing,
glasses clinking.
Crowds drunk,
heads bobbing,
eyes flapping,
perspiration dribbles
down a grinding dancer's spine.
Good times, veil sorrows.

Nature

Extinction

Winter strips towering timbers naked.
Trunks sloughing off rhytidome crusts
grayed and shedding with age.
Pale splashes of emerald spruce
sprout among burnt sienna.
Roots gnarled like mangled trellises,
choking, shriveling, shrinking breath.
Cracked torsos recline on frigid ground
atop undug graves.
Some cradled in arms of siblings,
some sagging, weighted down.
Sacred soil defiled, poisoned,
disfiguring, crippling.
Brittle limbs like broken hearts won't mend.
Statuesque timbers teetering,
toppling, disintegrating,
back into earth.

Evelyn White-Bey

Le'roi

They plucked him from
the muddy river
on a dreary damp
Sunday morning,
wrapped
in a heavy army-green tarp,
like a toddler's blanket
shielding a lifeless form.
Stench of seaweed
and decaying fish
floated hypnotically in the air.
Tingling nostrils.
The river sobbing as if remorseful
for its taking.
Murky waters
clutching a memory.
A bloated hand
tumbled out.
Pasty fingernails,
waterlogged flesh,
bleached like chalk against
a backdrop of dark bluish-white
storm clouds, threatening.
Half curved fingers,
a bloodless hand,
unmoving,
like stagnant clouds.
A hand, sinking in

spongy black moss
rested on a soggy
river bank.
An image
permanently
branded.

Evelyn White-Bey

Twilight

Upon autumn's meadow,
midnight indigo suspends overhead.
I am
a night-sky gazer,
witnessing twinkling galaxies,
Sirius,
Orion's belt,
Venus,
Pluto,
Regulus,
Cassiopeia,
unmanned stars and
the great SHE-moon,
deeply mystifying
and distant,
yet connected.
Dominant She energy
resurrects
a kinship, familiarity
at soul's center.
Opening awareness to
concede a higher
presence,
greater than I,
presiding over the cosmos.
A divine plan still evolving,
inspired by you and me.

Sunsets

Daylight wanes.
Flamingo sunsets
unveil a cosmic medley
of variegated oils,
passion pinks,
bohemian sables,
stately violets,
raspberry crimson,
dapper blues,
breathtaking hues,
garnish the heavens.
She moves eastward
before night falls,
drawing her cloak
closer to her bosom.
She sleeps.

Evelyn White-Bey

Summer

August heat,
fleshy heaviness,
stifling,
oppressive,
weighty upon me.
Beads of sweat bubble
over upper lip like blisters.
Dense, thick air
like tortoise clouds
barely moving.
I shuffle over
to the Adirondack chair.
Moist skin melting into
the warm, red varnished wood.
Inhaling
stagnant fragrance of gardenias,
numbing,
easing me into slumber.

Survivors

Without warning
the waters came
raging,
catching us unaware,
knocking over homes,
uprooting trees,
drowning livestock,
silencing tongues.
Though it ended quickly,
that was all it took
to wash away what many had built.
People crawled out of their
dark spaces,
shocked, stoic faces,
weeping women, children, fathers,
searching for what was --
was no more.

Evelyn White-Bey

Spirituality

Unshakable

Like
the apple tree
sometimes
weighted down by
heavy,
wormy,
ripe and
rotten apples,
bends
low
to Earth
but
unbreakable,
so should
our faith be;
pliable
yet
unwavering.

Evelyn White-Bey

Fears

I admit, God,
sometimes
I'm afraid
of roaring thunder.
I tremble when lightning flashes,
scramble beneath covers,
crawl under a bed,
hide in a closet,
because, God,
I don't understand it all,
though fear has no place
inside of You.
Still I forget
Your awesomeness,
Your power.

Beliefs

I believe
　　　in me.
I believe in family values,
　　　they serve as guideposts of mindfulness.
I believe in miracles
　　　because I am one.
I believe in pots of gold at the end of rainbows.
　　　I'll someday uncover it.
I believe in life after death.
　　　Life is a semi-colon, never a period.
I believe in hugs and kisses when we greet.
　　　We don't do that enough.
I believe in good mornings and good nights.
　　　Every moment should be celebratory.
I believe in angels
　　　and other stuff I can't explain or see.
I believe in poetry that doesn't rhyme.
　　　Poetry has a language of its own.
I believe in today,
　　　for today is creating my tomorrows.
I believe.
I believe in me.

Evelyn White-Bey

Telescope

God's telescope,
        summoning closer,
        life magnified,
        perceiving
        mountains, horizons and
        far out spaces,
        even moons, stars, galaxies,
        some yet to be revealed.
God's telescope,
        shrinking worries,
        problems
        with tampering of knobs
        increasing, decreasing,
        expanding, contracting,
        never
        disappearing from view.
God's telescope,
        from a distance
        appearing miniature,
        then widening
        in
        periphery
        and depth,
        intensified.

God's telescope,
　　　stripping blinders,
　　　rolling back veils
　　　of maya,
　　　through Spirit's lens,
　　　yet never withdrawing from
　　　the sanctuary of self.

Evelyn White-Bey

Idols

Gods—
created in
personal images.
Ivory, beige, ebony, red, yellow,
resting on altars, mantles,
motionless, speechless, blind, dumb.
Bowing, paying homage
to lifeless idols
without breath, or
consciousness.
Created gods,
ivory, beige, ebony, red, and yellow
trophies,
lifeless,
soulless,
decorated spaces
of inanimate objects.
Images of nothing
invented through
warped egos.

Transformation

Not so long ago
I worried about what
people thought of me.
Now
I think about dying,
when, where, and how it will happen,
when I exhale my last breath and
shut my eyes
to physical existence.
Without physical
encumbrances,
my sight and
other senses amplified,
I will walk beside my loved ones.
They will be unaware
of my presence.
I will whisper "I love you"
tenderly in their ears,
they will think it a dream.
I will guide them along,
bestowing blessings.
They will believe them
to be mere coincidences.
I will plant memories in them
to remember me.
They will think
them imaginary.

Evelyn White-Bey

Incarnation

Souls
seem lost,
stumbling,
picking, tossing back pebbles,
falling,
won't stay down.
Finding their way
through life's intricate mazes
amid thorny and weedy trails,
voyaging across
mossy vales, rocky trails,
seizing flashes of solitude,
embracing nature.
Inhaling honeysuckle blossoms,
biting overripe persimmons,
savoring sprigs of mint julep,
sipping sweet, red Moscato.
Simple soul wanderings.

Immortality

Such thoughts rarely entered my mind,
that someday I would no longer breathe
or occupy a physical body.
Living, my only priority, demanded attention.
Newspapers highlighted passing
with sugar coated scripts and accomplishments,
now gone to some far-off abode
beyond human perception.
Ah, years I thought it would be
before I joined those weary travelers
who stared from black and white pages
with dated photographs.
But
it did come,
in twilight of autumn
where trees dressed up in effervescent hues,
where sunsets flamed luminously across
canvassed pale blues and cotton candy clouds,
morning breezes crisp and chilled.
It came quietly; no bells, horns, or jingles.
Unnoticed almost.
A shadowy figure pressed against me,
tender warm fingers pricked my countenance.
Then I knew time had ceased.
Briefly I knew not that I had left.
There were no goodbyes.
Everything seemed as it was:
the walls of my room, the bedroom quilt

Evelyn White-Bey

my grandmother made with
scrawny arthritic fingers.
The same house at the edge of a preserved forest.
I seemed as I always did,
except
my senses were altered somehow,
smothered, choked, stilled,
like a smoke-filled room.
Death accompanied me like a
vaporous shadow,
neither smiling nor frowning,
intent on its task,
grasping my hand, leading me
from a place of familiarity
to the unknown.
I was not quite ready;
I tried to negotiate.
Not to be. My exit was fixed.
Like the moon in the heavenly spheres,
it would not be undone.
As I looked upon
my loved ones,
whom I imagined would miss me,
a sense of remorse heavily engulfed me.
In a final feeble effort, I reached out
to caution them,
but words remained unspoken
upon dead lips and sealed ears,

separated by an invisible veil,
frozen in death's embrace.
The Earth shrank as we traveled
further into foreign realms,
though somehow familiar,
a vague sense of calm caressed me.
Physicality ceased,
death had come.
Never too soon.

Evelyn White-Bey

Past to Present Journeying

Sometimes, when all is quiet, I reflect on the person I used to be, from a baby, a toddler, a teenager, a young adult, to where I am now. I wonder about my past lives and how they played a role in my present situation. I think about my formative years in the south. I think about my college years–metaphysical studies in which I spent years learning the cosmos, the occult, and spirituality while trying to understand who I was. Still I do not know who I am.

I think about the people I love and loved; the people whom I no longer see or hear from anymore. I wonder where they are and what they are doing. I think of those who no longer inhabit physical bodies. Where are they? Do they think about me? I miss them.

I think about the little girl who was so afraid to attend school—in the first grade, she cried every day; or the teenager who had no confidence at all and pretended to be all the other people she saw and fantasized about on TV and in magazines. I think about my periods of escapism from reality, like diving headfirst into poetry. The world then was an intimidating place. I think about inherited fears, imprinted upon me too early by an alcoholic father and a struggling mother, fears that trickled down to my siblings and me. I think about the closeness of family; how secure I felt when I sat between my mother's legs as she braided my hair. I think about the good, quiet days when Dad was sober.

I think about my first yoga teacher, who was awesome and taught me much about the complexities of life. At the time, though, I felt I was too young to be spiritual, disciplined, and into meditation and metaphysics, so I drifted away to the party scene, only to return years later.

I think about the shy little girl who was afraid to talk to boys, so she read Harlequin romance novels. I remember my first heartbreak; I thought the pain would kill me, but it did not. I think about my past choices because those choices have brought me here. Who was that person in that body not so long ago? Where has that person gone? Who am I?

I think about the times when I sat and gossiped about other people because they did not think, look, act, or dress like me. I think about how opinionated I used to be. I hated the fact that people did not view life as I did. I thought I was right, you know, I really did. I think whether growing up in poverty—dirt poor in the South—was a good thing. Did it benefit or impede me? What did it teach? Have I released all the pent up hatred and anger I carried as a child, a child who suffered discrimination and racial woes? Or the child who had no voice because children were to be seen, not heard?

I remember auditioning for a speech in high school, and although I studied diligently and rehearsed my lines, when it was my turn to speak, I stuttered, muttered, fluttered, and could not remember anything. The audience snickered and giggled at my blubbering. I wondered whether everybody would always view me as flawed; not good enough to be special, that anybody could love. I kept all my emotions bottled up inside, fermenting like homemade wine.

I remember when I could eat anything and not gain a pound, or worry about cholesterol or high blood pressure or any of the other human-created illnesses. I remember when I played basketball for hours, played from sun-up to sundown, I never had aches or pains. Boredom was a foreign word.

I remember all the things I did not receive although I prayed fervently for them. I remember the strict teachings and "non-dating" at seventeen. There was no hanging out with friends and boyfriends. However, with my wild and vivid imagination, I did all those things, they did not have to be real.

Poverty was a persistent shadow. I was fed fresh food from home-grown gardens and slaughtered chickens and pigs; clothed by magic hands that knew how to work a sewing machine; housed in rickety homes with leaky roofs, creaky porches, and strange live-in critters, yet loved by family and extended families. I can say I appreciate the values and morals my parents taught me, although I did not appreciate the lessons until I was well into adulthood.

Santa did not visit every year. I cared less that he was make-believe, a story fabricated by grown-ups. Albeit a lie, somehow it still made a little girl jump for joy, pain temporarily forgotten.

I think about my early working years when I thought I knew it all. I think about the young woman who filed grievance after grievance because her co-workers were bigots, jackasses; she stood up and challenged them. I think about the revolutionary and militant woman I used to be. No, you could not tell me what to do.

I remember saying as a little girl that when I grew up, I would never live in the "dirty, rotten" South. Now I want to move back.

I think about my family, those who have transitioned; my grandparents, my father, my brother, my niece, uncles, aunts. Do they think of me? Or have they forgotten? I think of them; sometimes I dream about them.

I think about the material trinkets I have accumulated over the years. My books—what can I say about my books that clutter my space? My books—maybe I am too attached to them. What is so complicated about letting stuff go? Worn sweaters, jeans, shoes (too small, but they look *good*). Or the watch that has not had a battery in, say, ten years. Or the ten to twenty-year-old store receipts, bills, and tax returns. For what? What purpose do any of these things serve us in our spiritual evolution?

Would we not breathe a sigh of relief if our personal spaces—outer and inner—were less cluttered? Would not our lives become happier, more serene and less toxic if we let go of attachments? Do these things reflect who we are? I ask myself, "Who will I be if I get rid of all my stuff? Who will I be if I keep it?"

Sometimes, I think about tomorrow; what does it hold? Am I making the right choices today to create a positive future? Mostly, I try to live in the present moment; right now is all I have. That is where God is.

My soul whispers,
I am changing.
I am becoming.
I am evolving.
into something
phenomenal.
My soul declares,
I am living.
I am loving
I am dancing.
to descants of
the Divine.
I am alive.
I Am.

~ ~ ~ ~ ~ ~